Fast Food
for
Two

Fast Food
for
Two

foulsham

LONDON • NEW YORK • TORONTO • SYDNEY

Contents

Know-how – makes quick cooking even quicker

It seems a contradiction, but it pays off: take your time when cooking, especially if you want it to be quick. Thirty minutes is usually sufficient, and can often be much less, when you keep strictly to the job in hand. The recipes are arranged in such a way that all the various tasks can be carried out one after another without wasting any time. In this way everything will go without a hitch!

Useful kitchen equipment

Knives which can no longer chop onions, pepper mills which deliver only microscopic portions at each twist, and saucepans which take an eternity to cook anything – such tools are sand in the kitchen gears. This is why you should always buy good quality equipment!

Knives: A good, sharp professional knife is the best tool in the kitchen: it should have a heavy handle and be comfortable to hold. The blade shaft should extend well inside the handle itself and be fixed securely. Such knives are not cheap, but they will last a lifetime if you take care of them, for example do not put them in a dishwasher (this is how the blades are scratched and nicked), but wash and dry them immediately after use.

Pots and pans: A stainless steel or enamelled steel pan looks good, is durable and has a professional look. It should have a thick, so-called 'sandwich' base, with a copper layer in between or another good heat conductor, because steel on its own does not conduct heat well. Close-fitting lids (glass lids are practical) save up to half the time and energy. Heat-resistant handles means you do not have to transfer ingredients from one pan to another for some recipes (for example, when vegetables are steamed on top of the cooker and then gratinéed in the oven).

Two pans, by the way, are always better than one. Then in the case of large (T-bone) steaks, escalopes, croquettes or omelettes, two portions can be cooked at the same time, instead of one after another.

Electric blender: It minces, grates, liquidizes and purées almost anything that needs cutting up small in no time at all: thick bunches of herbs to mix with quark or make a pesto, onions, garlic, cheese, nuts and chocolate along with fruit and vegetables. Even meat can be turned into wonderfully fresh minced (ground) meat or tartar, and you can make special types of minced meat yourself, for example from lamb or poultry, or use a fresh fish fillet to make a luxurious salmon tartar.

Food processor: This is something you cannot do without, because in one operation it is possible to mince, purée, beat and mix. For small quantities you should also have an additional small-sized bowl. And most important: find a firm place on the work surface to install your food processor. It wastes time if you always have to take it out of the cupboard and assemble it.

Hand blender with cutter: This is required over and above the food processor, and can be used directly in the saucepan to stir, purée or beat. The electric socket for this machine should be as near as possible to the cooker.

Cutting board: Here we recommend a board which is as large as possible (so that nothing slips over the side), and preferably made of plastic so that it can be cleaned hygienically in a dishwasher.

Salad spinner: It will turn a dripping wet lettuce into a crispy dry one in seconds, which will assimilate the dressing more easily. It is also ideal for drying herbs.

Colander and sieves: You should have a number of these in different sizes because there is always something to drain or pour away. Wire baskets save space and can be hung from hooks either over the sink or under the wall cupboards.

Kitchen scales and measures: More important than a stylish design is an accurate scale which is easy-to-read. You should always be able to turn the scales back to zero by hand, even when there is something in the bowl. In this way exact amounts can be added. To measure minute quantities, small measuring containers made of stainless steel are practical (a set of four is available from 6 to 25 cl/ 2 to 8 fl oz). A small amount of butter or chocolate can be melted in them or gelatine dissolved over warm water. It is even quicker to note a few of the spoon and cup measurements.

Garlic press: Buy a press which takes unpeeled cloves and quickly removes the peel by means of tiny cleaning teeth.

Pepper mill: Mills with handles look rather old-fashioned, but are far more practical than those with a head that turns. Make sure the opening where it is filled is large enough, so that this operation does not become a test of your patience.

Spice grater: The most effective has a long handle which you can hold firmly. They are actually designed for Parmesan cheese, but are equally suitable for grating nutmeg, other cheeses and lemon rind – for anything, in fact, that you need to grate over a saucepan or a plate. Also useful is a normal kitchen grater with fine holes. Mini spice graters, on the other hand, are awkward and best avoided altogether.

Helpful basic products for cooking

Without ready-made products it is impossible to work properly if you want to cook quickly. You will want to avoid ingredients which need long simmering but still have enough choice and scope to conjure up special dishes for the table in no time.

Meat and vegetable stock: You will need this for soups, sauces, ragouts and many other dishes. The most practical method is to use instant stock, which can be measured out exactly spoon by spoon. You should always have two types available: a light chicken or vegetable stock and a heavy beef stock. For fish dishes you should use either pure vegetable or chicken stock, or mix one of them with white wine or a little lemon juice. By the way: instant stock powder is useful for seasoning – instead of salt!

Frozen herbs and vegetables: These are the best alternative when fresh food is not available or when fresh vegetables look past their best on the shelf. The large deep-freeze companies process the food next to the fields in which the vegetables are grown, so that everything is as fresh as possible and few of the vitamins are lost.

Important: frozen vegetables should be cooked as briefly as possible, so they remain crispy. The times for cooking given on the packets can generally be halved, and shortened even further if the contents have been partly defrosted.

For tender frozen peas it is often sufficient simply to pour hot water over them in a sieve. In the case of frozen broccoli – and fresh – cut the florets from the stalks, cook the stalks first and finally cook the florets for 1-2 minutes. This prevents the florets becoming mushy. Of particular use are frozen soup vegetables. A small packet cooked in a stock or soup produces a flavour as wonderfully full and aromatic as that obtained from fresh vegetables, without any of the time-consuming preparation. Should you wish to bind a light sauce, cook it with the soup vegetables, finally purée and pass through a sieve. The sauce then becomes thick and you save on calories!

Frozen puff pastry: This makes quick cooking child's play. After brief defrosting one can make, for example, crispy cheese sticks or horns, or pastry pockets with a sweet or savoury filling. The pastry can also be cleverly used to wrap meat (beef Wellington) or to produce an elegant soup. Simply roll out the dough, cut out a circle, fasten it with egg white to the edge of the heatproof tureen or bowl and bake in the oven at 200°C/400°F/gas mark 6 until light brown and crispy.

Chilled fresh pastry: This is even quicker and easier to use than frozen dough. It is also available made with wholemeal flour.

Canned tomatoes: Besides pulses and sweetcorn, there are many kinds of canned vegetables that should not be overlooked. Canned tomatoes are especially practical and good value for use in soups and sauces. They often taste better than fresh tomatoes,

when you cannot obtain really ripe fruit. Sieved or coarsely chopped tomatoes in cartons are also to be recommended. They can be bought already seasoned just in case you need to produce a dish really quickly.

Quick-cooking rice: It is an ideal accompaniment because it can always be cooked at the same time as other ingredients and it never fails. With the addition of various spices, cheese or mushrooms, it can be used to set the tone for the main dish.

Mashed potato from a packet: This can hardly be distinguished from the mashed potato you make yourself, as long as it is not made too thick and fresh milk is used with some butter or cream and a pinch of nutmeg. For a change beat in some soft cheese or herb quark – this adds spice to the mashed potato.

On balance: If you look at ready-made products and prepared produce, such as frozen vegetables or canned tomatoes, not as the end product, but as a starting point for your own creativity, then you will be able to work miracles in the kitchen!

The best tips and professional tricks from A to Z

Apples, pears and celery: If you intend to eat these raw, grate them into a bowl containing some lemon juice. in this way they will not discolour.

Bacon: If the bacon is blanched just before frying, it will be crispier and less salty.

Butter: Hard butter from the refrigerator becomes soft quickly if cut into cubes with a large knife or covered with a basin warmed with hot water.

Cheese for gratin: If you add a few breadcrumbs (ratio 4 to 1) to the grated cheese the crust will become a lovely golden-brown.

Desserts: An effective form of decoration is to sprinkle strips of orange or lemon rind over the top. Use a grater (obtainable in household stores) on unwaxed fruit. A pretty effect is achieved by sieving cocoa powder (unsweetened chocolate) or icing (confectioner's) sugar on the plate first.

Eggs: They are much easier to shell under cold running water.

Whisked eggs: When beating eggs the whisk should always be spotlessly clean and especially free of fat. Always whip the white of an egg before the yolk, then it will not be necessary to rinse the whisk in between.

Fat for frying and roasting: It must be extremely hot, otherwise it takes ages for the food to become crispy on the outside. To test the temperature, hold a cocktail stick (toothpick) in the fat or throw in a cube of bread. If the fat forms little bubbles around it, you can begin your frying.

Garlic cloves: The green shoot in the centre of the clove should always be removed because it tastes bitter.

Herbs: The leaves can most easily be removed by rubbing your fingers down the stalk against the way the leaves lie, that is to say, from the tip to the base. This trick works especially well with thyme, marjoram, tarragon, oregano and rosemary.

Lemon juice: If you only need a few drops for seasoning, hold a sieve under half a lemon when squeezing to prevent pips falling into the food.

Meat: This should preferably be purchased the day before you intend to use it, then brush it with oil, cover and place in the refrigerator. It becomes wonderfully tender!

Mushrooms: These are quickly cleaned if the stalks are first removed (this is where most of the dirt lies), the mushrooms are rinsed in water and shaken vigorously. Never leave mushrooms in water for long, because they soak up the water and then taste dreadful.

Noodles: They will be guaranteed to stay 'al dente' if you shorten the cooking time given on the packet to about 2 minutes, then turn off the heat and allow the noodles to stand for another 2 minutes in the water. Now and then take out a noodle to try it.

Onions and garlic cloves: A serrated (tomato) knife makes it much easier to peel both, because it grips the skin better. Shallots should be scalded quickly before peeling, then the skins almost always come off by themselves.

Chopped onions: If you want to keep them, mix them with a little oil and keep in an airtight jar in the refrigerator. Otherwise they will oxidize and taste bitter.

Oyster mushrooms: If possible choose small ones, because they do not need so much preparation and they are considerably more tender than the larger ones.

Parmesan and other cheeses to be grated: Freeze the cheese in small pieces and grate frozen as required. This method makes them especially light and flaky.

Cooking potatoes: If you have only a short time in which to cook them, peel the potatoes (the larger the better), and cut into dice. This way they will be cooked in about 5 minutes. Or you can fry the diced potatoes in a frying pan (skillet) until crispy; oil is best for this together with a couple of fresh sprigs of herbs (rosemary, thyme). You will then have sautéed potatoes, which are so well loved in French cooking. Diced potatoes can also then be cooked with other vegetables. This is an excellent way of making a soup base as the starch they release will cause a slight thickening of the stock.

Rice: If you want to serve other types of rice from time to time (e.g. scented or wild rice), cook a large amount all at once, then freeze it in individual portions. The rice can then be steamed quickly to defrost, then warmed.

Salads: Mix the salad dressing in the salad bowl itself, cross the salad spoons over the bowl and place the salad ingredients in a heap on top. Mix the salad just before serving and it will not go limp.

Escalopes: Before frying, toss the meat in a little flour and beat it well to tenderize it. The escalopes will then be crispy and remain juicy.

Vegetables: These cook quicker without salt in the water. Fashionable at the moment are julienned vegetables. To make them, use a peeler to cut carrots, kohlrabi or celery into thin strips and cook for a short time in water. Cleaned vegetables remain fresh if you immerse them (perhaps also cut up small) in water soured with a little lemon juice or vinegar. The vegetables take on a slightly sour taste and so are ideal for Chinese dishes.

Notes on the recipes

As the **preparation time** of most of the dishes is usually not longer than 30 minutes, times are not included. The recipes are for **two portions**; however, the **calories** relate to one portion. Usually quantities given in the recipes relate to **uncooked food**, so those amounts can be put on your shopping list when you buy the produce. **Spoon quantities** generally refer to lightly heaped spoons.

Useful to know

6 medium potatoes = about 500 g/1 lb
5 medium apples = about 500 g/1 lb
5 medium tomatoes = about 500 g/1 lb
1 lemon produces about 45 ml/3 tbsp juice
1 orange produces 100 ml/3½ fl oz/
6½ tbsp juice

Salads
and
Soups

Rice Salad with Papaya and Prawns

100 g/4 oz/½ cup quick-cooking rice

1 stick celery

1 small papaya

100 g/4 oz peeled prawns

juice of 1 orange
15 ml/1 tbsp white wine vinegar
15 ml/1 tbsp olive oil
15 ml/1 tbsp mayonnaise
5 ml/1 tsp medium-hot mustard,
sugar, cayenne pepper, salt and freshly
ground pepper

1. To cook the rice, follow the instructions on the packet.
2. Meanwhile clean the stick of celery, pull off the strings, wash and cut diagonally into slices.
3. Peel the papaya and halve along the length. Cut off both ends. Remove the seeds with a spoon and discard. Cut the papaya halves once more in two along the length, then cut diagonally into thin slices.
4. Quickly rinse the prawns in a colander. To make a creamy dressing, mix together the orange juice, vinegar, olive oil, mayonnaise, mustard, sugar and spices.
5. In a bowl, mix the drained rice, celery, papaya and prawns with the dressing.

about 480 kcal/2000 kJ

Frisée Lettuce with Beef Fillet

1 small frisée lettuce

4 cloves garlic

200 g/7 oz beef fillet

75 ml/5 tbsp olive oil

salt and freshly ground pepper

30 ml/2 tbsp red wine vinegar

2.5 ml/½ tsp herb mustard

1. Clean the frisée lettuce, wash, spin dry and tear into walnut-sized pieces.
2. Peel the garlic cloves and cut into thin slices. Cut the beef fillet into thin strips.
3. Heat 30 ml/2 tbsp of the oil in a frying pan (skillet) and cook the garlic until golden-brown. Remove and drain on absorbent kitchen paper.
4. Stir-fry the meat on each side in the garlic juices for about 1 minute on a high heat. Remove and season.
5. To make the dressing, mix the remaining oil, vinegar and mustard, and season. Toss the lettuce in the dressing.
6. Put the lettuce on a plate and sprinkle with the beef fillet and garlic slices.

about 310 kcal/1300 kJ

Raw Salad with Celeriac, Apple and Beetroot

60-75 ml/4-5 tbsp single (light) cream

1 pinch sugar

60 ml/4 tbsp lemon juice

salt and freshly ground pepper

100 g/4 oz celeriac

1 small beetroot (beet), cooked

1 cooking (tart) apple

15 g/½ oz/2 tbsp walnut pieces

1. For the salad dressing, mix the cream with the sugar and half the lemon juice, and season.

2. Peel the celeriac and beetroot. Peel the apple, quarter and core.

3. Coarsely grate the celeriac and apple with the salad grater and mix with the remaining lemon juice. Grate the beetroot into another bowl.

4. Set aside four large pieces of walnut for decoration. Coarsely chop the rest and add to the celeriac and apple mixture.

5. Arrange the celeriac and apple salad on two plates with the beetroot in the centre of each. Pour the cream dressing over the salad and garnish with the remaining walnuts.

about 210 kcal/880 kJ

Piquant Vegetable Salad

---

1 egg

½ cucumber

---

1 tomato

---

1 red (bell) pepper

---

1 red onion

---

5 ml/1 tsp paprika paste
5 ml/1 tsp medium-hot mustard
5 ml/1 tsp lemon juice
salt and freshly ground pepper
1 pinch sambal oelek (hot chilli paste)

---

4 slices crispbread

---

1. Hard boil (hard cook) the egg for about 10 minutes. Rinse in cold water, shell and dice finely (preferably with an egg cutter).
2. Wash the cucumber and tomato. Dice both finely.
3. Wash the pepper and halve. Remove the seeds and inner white skin. Then dice the flesh finely.
4. Peel the onion and dice finely. Carefully mix the egg, cucumber, tomato, pepper and onion in a bowl.
5. Make a paste of the paprika, mustard, lemon juice, salt, pepper and sambal oelek and mix into the salad.
6. Serve the vegetable salad with the crispbread.

about 180 kcal/752 kJ

Noodle Salad with Salmon

100 g/4 oz plain or green noodles, salt

1 salmon cutlet,
15 ml/1 tbsp lemon juice

15 ml/1 tbsp wine vinegar
30 ml/2 tbsp orange juice
30 ml/2 tbsp olive oil
5 ml/1 tsp medium-hot mustard
freshly ground pepper
cayenne pepper

½ bunch each chives, dill and parsley

1. Cook the noodles in salted water until 'al dente'. Rinse in cold water through a sieve and drain well.
2. Meanwhile, gently simmer the salmon cutlet in water for 3-4 minutes. Remove from the water. Remove the medium-sized bones and as many of the finer ones as possible; remove the skin. Sprinkle the salmon with the lemon juice.
3. To make the dressing, stir the vinegar, orange juice, oil, mustard and the spices together.
4. Wash the herbs, shake dry, chop finely and add to the dressing.
5. Mix the noodles and the dressing. Divide the salmon into walnut-sized pieces and toss in the salad.

about 450 kcal/1880 kJ

Rocket Salad with Mozzarella

200 g/7 oz mozzarella, 60 ml/4 tbsp balsamic vinegar, 30 ml/2 tbsp lemon juice, 60 ml/4 tbsp olive oil, salt and freshly ground pepper, 1 pinch sugar

150 g/5 oz rocket lettuce or leaf spinach

4 tomatoes, 1 small can sweetcorn

1. Slice the mozzarella. To make the dressing, mix together the vinegar, lemon juice, oil, salt, pepper and sugar. Add the sliced mozzarella.

2. Wash the rocket or leaf spinach, clean, spin dry and pluck the leaves into walnut-sized pieces.
3. Wash and quarter the tomatoes; drain the sweetcorn well.
4. Add the rocket or spinach, quartered tomatoes and sweetcorn to the mozzarella and mix well.

about 475 kcal/1990 kJ

Melon Salad
with Ham

1 small Lollo rosso lettuce
½ cucumber
1 small Galia or Ogen melon
15 ml/1 tbsp raspberry vinegar, 1 pinch salt, 1 pinch sugar, 30 ml/2 tbsp oil, freshly ground pepper
50 g/2 oz Parma ham slices

1. Clean the lettuce, wash quickly and spin dry. Tear into walnut-sized pieces and place in a bowl.
2. Peel the cucumber, halve along the length and remove the seeds with a spoon. Slice the cucumber very thinly.
3. Cut the melon into eight segments and remove the seeds. Cut the skin from the melon segments. Finally cut the fruit flesh diagonally into thin slices.
4. Add the cucumber and melon to the salad bowl. To make the dressing, stir together the vinegar, salt, sugar and oil, and pour over the salad. Mix everything gently and grind a little pepper over the top.
5. Cut the Parma ham into small pieces and toss in the salad.

about 310 kcal/1300 kJ

Dandelion Salad
with Tomatoes and Bacon

75 g/3 oz dandelion leaves (or lamb's lettuce), 3 tomatoes
15 ml/1 tbsp lemon juice, 15 ml/1 tbsp balsamic vinegar, 15 ml/1 tbsp walnut oil, 15 ml/1 tbsp sunflower oil, salt and freshly ground pepper, 1 pinch sugar
6 rashers (slices) streaky bacon

1. Clean the dandelion or lamb's lettuce, wash and spin dry. Wash and quarter the tomatoes.
2. To make the dressing, mix the lemon juice, vinegar, oil, salt, pepper and sugar.
3. In a frying pan, fry the bacon without fat until crispy. Place on absorbent kitchen paper to drain.
4. Turn the dandelion or lamb's lettuce and the tomato in the dressing. Arrange the bacon on top.

about 230 kcal/960 kJ

Cheese Salad with Courgettes and Radishes

250 g/9 oz piece of Gouda or Edam cheese

1 large courgette (zucchini), 1 bunch radishes

30 ml/2 tbsp sherry vinegar
15 ml/1 tbsp sherry
30 ml/2 tbsp oil
5 ml/1 tsp medium-hot mustard
salt and freshly ground pepper
Worcestershire sauce

1 bunch each flat-leafed parsley and chives

1. Remove the rind from the cheese and cut into 1 cm/½ in cubes.

2. Wash the courgette, clean and cut into sticks about 4 cm/1½in long and the thickness of a pencil. Clean the radishes, wash and quarter.

3. To make the dressing, in a bowl mix the sherry vinegar, sherry, oil, mustard, salt and pepper and a dash of Worcestershire sauce.

4. Add the cheese, courgette and radishes, and mix everything well.

5. Wash the parsley and chives, shake dry and chop finely. Mix into the salad.

about 595 kcal/2490 kJ

Fennel and Grapefruit Salad

salt, 2 small fennel bulbs

15 ml/1 tbsp honey, 15 ml/1 tbsp soy sauce, 200 g/7 oz turkey steaks, freshly ground pepper

45 ml/3 tbsp oil

1 pink grapefruit

15 ml/1 tbsp vinegar, 15 ml/1 tbsp medium sherry, 5 ml/1 tsp honey, cayenne pepper

Tabasco sauce, 4 slices baguette

1. Bring enough salted water to cook the fennel to the boil. Wash the fennel, cut away the fennel fronds and place on one side. Halve the bulbs and cut out the stalk with a wedge-shaped cut. Cut the fennel into very narrow strips or grate coarsely with a kitchen slicer.

2. Boil the fennel strips in the water for about 3 minutes. Rinse through a sieve under cold water and leave to drain well.

3. Mix the honey with the soy sauce. Coat the turkey steaks on both sides with this mixture, then season with pepper.

4. Heat 15 ml/1 tbsp of the oil in a frying pan (skillet) and fry the turkey steaks on each side for 3-4 minutes. Remove from the pan, season with salt and leave to cool slightly.

5. Take as much of the thick peel off the grapefruit as you can, then cut the grapefruit into slices, quarter and cut out any remaining white skin.

6. Make the dressing with the vinegar, sherry, honey, the remaining oil and the cayenne pepper, season with salt and pepper.

7. Cut the turkey steaks into strips and mix with the fennel. Pour the dressing over the salad, season well with Tabasco sauce and finally fold in the grapefruit pieces. Chop up the fennel fronds and sprinkle over the salad. Serve together with the baguette.

about 420 kcal/1750 kJ

Frisée Soup with Dumplings

---

1 small frisée lettuce

---

1 small onion, 15 ml/1 tbsp butter or margarine

---

500 ml/17 fl oz/2¼ cups vegetable stock (instant), salt and freshly ground pepper, 1 pinch sugar

---

30 ml/2 tbsp lemon juice, 15 ml/1 tbsp sherry, Hungarian paprika powder

---

100 g/4 oz sausagemeat

---

100 g/4 oz/½ cup double (heavy) cream

---

1. Clean the lettuce, wash well and spin dry. Place the tiny yellow lettuce leaves on one side, and chop the rest coarsely.
2. Peel the onion, chop finely and fry in the hot butter for 2-3 minutes, then add the chopped lettuce and let it wilt for 2-3 minutes.
3. Add the vegetable stock. Season with salt, pepper and sugar, and leave to simmer for about 10 minutes. Pour the soup through a sieve, drain off the salad strips and discard.
4. Season the soup with lemon juice, sherry and a little paprika.
5. With your hands wet, shape the sausagemeat into dumplings and simmer in the soup for about 6 minutes.
6. Beat the cream until stiff and fold into the soup. Finally, add the yellow lettuce leaves and serve immediately.

about 350 kcal/1460 kJ

Broccoli Soup with Little Meat Balls

---

300 g/11 oz frozen broccoli, 5 ml/1 tsp salt, freshly ground pepper, nutmeg, 5 ml/1 tsp dried thyme

---

200 g/7 oz minced (ground) steak, 1 small egg, paprika

---

30 ml/2 tbsp crème fraîche

---

1. Bring the broccoli to the boil in a saucepan with 500 ml/17 fl oz/2¼ cups of water, the salt, a little pepper and nutmeg and the thyme, and leave to simmer on a low heat for about 10 minutes.
2. Knead the meat in a bowl with the egg. Season well with salt, pepper and paprika.
3. With wet hands, shape the meat into little dumplings. Place on a plate and set aside.
4. Remove the soup from the heat, stir in the crème fraîche and purée with a hand blender.
5. Add the little meat balls. Simmer everything for a further 10 minutes on a low heat.
6. Season the broccoli soup once more with salt, pepper and nutmeg.

about 250 kcal/1040 kJ

Leek Soup with Chicken and Bean Sprouts

---

400 g/14 oz leeks, 15 ml/1 tbsp sesame oil

---

500 ml/17 fl oz/2¼ cups chicken stock (instant)

---

200 g/7 oz chicken breast fillet

---

some freshly grated root ginger, soy sauce, white wine vinegar, sugar, cayenne pepper and salt

---

25 g/1 oz bean sprouts

---

1. Cut away the dark green part of the leek. Cut the rest of the leek along the length into two, wash under running water and drain well, then cut into narrow strips. Heat the oil in a saucepan and fry the leek.
2. Add the chicken stock and bring to the boil. Then cook the leek in the stock on a medium heat for about 15 minutes.
3. Wash the chicken breast fillet, pat dry and cut into walnut-sized pieces. Add to the leek soup and cook for a few minutes.
4. Season the soup with ginger, soy sauce, vinegar, sugar, cayenne pepper and salt.
5. Rinse the bean sprouts under hot water, drain, and warm for a short time in the soup.

about 220 kcal/920 kJ

Avocado Soup with Prawns

1 spring onion (scallion), 5 ml/1 tsp butter or margarine

500ml/17 fl oz/2¼ cups chicken stock (instant)

1 ripe avocado

50 g/2 oz/¼ cup cream, 100 g/4 oz peeled prawns (shrimps)

juice of ½ lemon, 15 ml/1 tbsp orange juice, Worcestershire sauce, salt, freshly ground pepper, cayenne pepper, 1 pinch sugar

1 bunch dill (dill weed)

1. Clean the spring onion, wash and chop finely. Heat the butter in a saucepan and fry the onion.

2. Add the chicken stock and leave to simmer for about 5 minutes.

3. Peel the avocado, remove the stone and dice the flesh finely. Off the heat, add the avocado to the soup and purée with a hand blender.

4. Add the cream and prawns to the soup and leave for a few minutes on a low heat.

5. Season the soup with lemon and orange juice, Worcestershire sauce, salt, pepper, cayenne pepper and sugar.

6. Wash the dill, shake dry, chop finely and sprinkle over the avocado.

about 370 kcal/1550 kJ

Snacks

Stuffed Red Peppers

2 red (bell) peppers

100 g/4 oz/½ cup feta cheese, 1 bunch dill (dill weed), 2 tomatoes, 50 g/2 oz/½ cup mushrooms

15 ml/1 tbsp lemon juice,
15 ml/1 tbsp olive oil,
salt and freshly ground pepper,
1 pinch sugar

1. Wash the peppers, halve along the length, remove the seeds, stalk and white skin.
2. Dice the feta cheese. Wash the dill, shake dry and chop finely. Wash the tomatoes and dice small. Clean the mushrooms and slice. Place the cheese, dill, tomatoes and mushrooms in a bowl.
3. Mix the lemon juice, oil, salt, pepper and sugar to make a dressing. Pour the dressing over the cheese mixture, stir well together and use it to fill the pepper halves.

about 270 kcal/1130 kJ

Crudités with Yoghurt Dip

1 small radicchio lettuce

1 red and 1 yellow (bell) pepper

½ cucumber

2 cartons low-fat yoghurt,
5 ml/1 tsp medium-hot mustard,
5 ml/1 tsp grated horseradish, salt and freshly ground pepper, some grated rind of unwaxed lemon, 30 ml/2 tbsp orange juice, 30 ml/2 tbsp lemon juice

15 ml/1 tbsp capers, 1 bunch chives

1. Clean the radicchio, wash and spin dry. Tear into walnut-sized pieces.
2. Clean the peppers, wash and halve. Remove the seeds and white skin. Cut the halves into long strips about 1 cm/½ in wide.
3. Wash the cucumber, cut along the length and then once in the opposite direction. Remove the seeds with a spoon. Then cut the cucumber into 1 cm/½ in strips. Arrange the salad and vegetables on two plates.
4. In a bowl, mix the yoghurt with the mustard, horseradish, spices, lemon rind and citrus juices.
5. Chop the capers finely. Wash the chives, shake dry and cut into tiny rolls. Stir both into the dip.

about 160 kcal/670 kJ

Filled Avocados

1 ripe avocado

50 g/2 oz/¼ cup mild sheep's cheese, 6 black olives, 1 bunch parsley

30 ml/2 tbsp lemon juice, 15 ml/1 tbsp olive oil, salt and freshly ground pepper

2 slices white bread, 15 ml/1 tbsp butter

1. Halve the avocado along the length and remove the stone. Using a tablespoon, carefully loosen the flesh from the peel and dice small. Reserve the avocado halves.

2. Dice the sheep's cheese small and mix with the olives and the diced avocado. Wash the parsley, shake dry, and chop finely.
3. Stir together the parsley, lemon juice, oil, salt and pepper and carefully fold into the avocado and cheese mixture.

4. Fill the hollowed-out avocado halves with the mixture. Toast the slices of bread, spread with butter and serve with the avocados.

about 420 kcal/1750 kJ

Avocado and Apple Carpaccio

---

15 ml/1 tbsp capers,
1 bunch parsley

---

30 mi/2 tbsp vinegar,
2.5 ml/½ tsp medium-hot mustard,
salt and freshly ground pepper,
1 pinch sugar,
60 ml/4 tbsp oil

---

1 large cooking (tart) apple, 30 ml/2
tbsp lemon juice

---

1 ripe avocado

---

1. Chop the capers finely.
Wash the parsley, shake dry
and chop finely.
2. Mix the vinegar with the
mustard, salt and pepper,
sugar, parsley and capers, and
finally beat in the oil.
3. Peel the apple, halve and
remove the core. Cut the apple
into fine slices. Sprinkle
immediately with the lemon
juice.
4. Arrange the apple slices like
a fan in a circle on two plates.
5. Peel the avocado, halve,
remove the stone and cut the
halves across in thin slices.
6. Lay the avocado slices on
top of the apple slices and
sprinkle the dressing evenly
over the top.

about 390 kcal/1630 kJ

Piquant Meat with Tomato and Shallots

1 tomato, 2 shallots

1 preserved or 1 small fresh chilli pepper

250 g/8 oz minced (ground) steak, some lime or lemon juice, some Worcestershire sauce, salt and freshly ground pepper, 2 slices rye bread

1. Wash the tomato and peel the shallots. Dice both finely.
2. Halve the chilli pepper along the length and scrape out the seeds with a knife. Then dice the flesh finely.
3. Mash the meat with a fork. Mix in the tomato, shallots and chilli pepper. Season with lime or lemon juice, Worcestershire sauce, salt and pepper. Serve with the bread. A leaf salad goes well with this dish.

about 510 kcal/2130 kJ

Roast Beef with Salsa Verde

3 bunches flat-leafed parsley

1 medium-sized pickled gherkin, 5 ml/ 1 tsp capers, 15 ml/1 tbsp oil, 15 ml/1 tbsp lemon juice, salt

1 hard-boiled (hard-cooked) egg

2 slices wholemeal bread

butter or margarine for spreading

100 g/4 oz beef slices

1. Wash the parsley, shake dry, and finely chop in a food processor.
2. Dice the gherkin and purée with the capers, oil, lemon juice, salt and parsley into a smooth paste (salsa verde).
3. Shell the egg, dice finely (the quickest way is in an egg cutter) and sprinkle over the salsa verde.
4. Spread the slices of bread with butter or margarine, place the roast beef on them and serve with the salsa verde.

about 320 kcal/1340 kj

Filled Flat Bread

½ flat bread loaf

100 g/4 oz/1 cup mushrooms (fresh or canned)

1 onion, 1 bunch parsley

2 eggs,
salt and freshly ground pepper,
nutmeg

45 ml/3 tbsp butter

1. Preheat the oven to 240°C/ 475°F/gas mark 9. Bake the bread for about 5 minutes.
2. Meanwhile, clean the fresh mushrooms, or just drain the can of mushrooms.
3. Peel the onion and dice finely. Wash the parsley, shake dry and chop finely.
4. Beat the eggs with nutmeg, salt and pepper.
5. Heat 15 ml/1 tbsp of the butter in a frying pan and fry the onion gently for about 1 minute. Add the mushrooms and stir-fry for about 3 minutes. Season.
6. Add the eggs to the frying pan with the parsley and leave to thicken.
7. Halve the flat bread. With a sharp knife, cut into the middle of the bread to form pockets. Spread the cut surfaces with the rest of the butter and fill the bread with the mushroom scrambled egg.

about 410 kcal/1710 kJ

Wholemeal Rolls with Minced Meat

1 leek

100 g/4 oz minced (ground) pork,
salt and freshly ground pepper,
paprika

1 packet frozen dough for wholemeal rolls (sufficient for 4)

flour for sprinkling

1. Preheat the oven to 200°C/ 400°F/gas mark 6. Clean the leek, halve along the length, wash thoroughly under running water and pat dry. Then cut into fine strips.
2. In a bowl, mix the leek strips with the minced meat and season with salt, pepper and paprika.
3. Prepare the dough by following the instructions on the packet. Spread the leek and minced meat mixture evenly over the pieces of dough, roll up and fasten the ends firmly together.
4. Lay greaseproof paper on a baking tray. Place the bread rolls with the join underneath on the tray, make two diagonal cuts and sprinkle with flour.
5. Bake the bread rolls for 15-20 minutes on the middle shelf. Serve hot or cold.

about 350 kcal/1460 kJ

Pepper Piperade

1 large red (bell) pepper

100 g/4 oz spicy pork and beef sausage (kabanos)

30 ml/2 tbsp olive oil, 10 ml/2 tsp dried thyme

1 small bunch basil

4 eggs

salt and freshly ground pepper

1. Wash and halve the pepper. Remove the seeds and white skin, and dice finely. Cut the sausage into very thin slices.
2. Heat the oil in a large frying pan and fry the diced pepper and sausage slices together for about 5 minutes, then season with the thyme.
3. Meanwhile, tear the basil leaves from the stalks, wash and shake dry. Cut half the leaves into fine strips, set the rest aside.
4. Whisk the eggs and stir in the basil strips.
5. Pour the egg mixture over the pepper and cook on a gentle heat until firm, which will take about 6 minutes. Season with salt and pepper. Garnish with the remaining basil leaves.

about 360 kcal/1500 kJ

Fried Goat's Cheese

2 slices white bread

15 ml/1 tbsp butter or margarine

100 g/4 oz frisée lettuce, 15 ml/1 tbsp red wine vinegar, 60 ml/4 tbsp oil, 5 ml/1 tsp medium-hot mustard, salt and freshly ground pepper, 15 ml/1 tbsp lemon juice, 1 pinch sugar

150 g/5 oz round goat's cheese, 1 egg, breadcrumbs

1. Remove the crusts from the bread, dice and fry in the butter or margarine until golden-brown.
2. Clean the frisée lettuce, wash and spin dry and tear into walnut-sized pieces. For the dressing, stir together the vinegar, 45 ml/3 tbsp of the oil, mustard, salt and pepper, lemon juice and sugar.
3. Cut the goat's cheese into slices roughly 1 cm/½ in thick. Whisk the egg with a little salt and pepper. Cover the goat's cheese on all sides with egg, then with breadcrumbs.

4. Heat the remaining 15 ml/1 tbsp of oil in a frying pan and fry the goat's cheese on both sides for 1 minute.
5. Toss the lettuce in the dressing, arrange on two flat plates and sprinkle the fried bread cubes over the top. Lay the goat's cheese in the centre.

about 525 kcal/2190 kJ

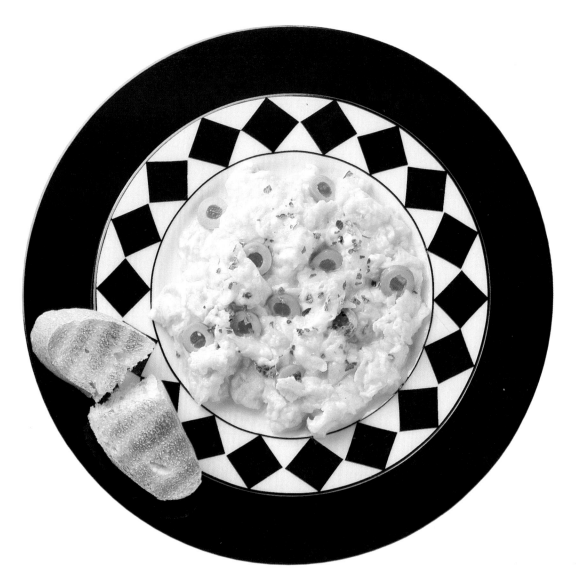

Scrambled Eggs
with Olives

3 eggs,
45 ml/3 tbsp milk,
5 ml/1 tsp paprika or tomato purée
(paste),
salt, Tabasco sauce

15 ml/1 tbsp butter or margarine

4 stuffed olives,
dried oregano

2 thin slices baguette,
½ clove garlic

1. Put the eggs into a bowl. Mix the paprika or tomato purée with the milk and beat into the eggs. Season with salt and Tabasco sauce.
2. Cut half of the butter or margarine into little flakes and stir into the egg mixture. Heat the remaining fat in a frying pan. Pour in the egg mixture and allow the egg to thicken, stirring constanly.

3. Cut the olives into rings and add to the eggs. Season the scrambled eggs with oregano.
4. Toast the baguette slices until golden-brown. Then rub them on one side with a peeled garlic clove and sprinkle with a little salt.
5. Serve the scrambled eggs with the baguette slices.

about 260 kcal/1090 kJ

Oyster Mushroom Saltimbocca

8 large or 16 small oyster mushrooms,
freshly ground pepper, 45 ml/3 tbsp
dried sage

8 thin slices Parma ham

30 ml/2 tbsp butter or margarine

4 crispbreads (or toast)

1. Clean the oyster
mushrooms, wash quickly and
dry with absorbent kitchen
paper. Sprinkle in pepper and
half of the sage.

2. Lay a slice of ham on each
mushroom (in the case of
small mushrooms, half a slice)
and skewer them together with
a cocktail stick (toothpick).
3. Heat the butter or the
margarine in a frying pan and
fry the mushrooms for 3-5
minutes first on the ham side,
then on the other. Sprinkle
with the rest of the sage. Serve
with the crispbread.

about 340 kcal/1420 kJ

Meat
and
Poultry

Strips of Meat with Herb Cream

2 pork escalopes, 3 cloves garlic

salt and freshly ground pepper,
5 ml/1 tsp dried oregano,
5 ml/1 tsp dried basil,
45 ml/3 tbsp oil

25 g/1 oz/2 tbsp soft cheese with herbs, 30 ml/2 tbsp soured (dairy sour) cream

½ cucumber

4 slices baguette

1. Cut the escalopes into fine strips and place in a bowl. Peel the garlic cloves and pass them through a garlic press.
2. Add the garlic, salt and pepper, oregano, basil and oil to the bowl and mix with the meat. Leave to stand for about 10 minutes.
3. Meanwhile mix the soft cheese with the soured cream and season with salt and pepper.
4. Wash the cucumber and slice.
5. On a high heat, stir-fry the marinaded meat in a frying pan, stirring continuously. Serve together with the herb cream, the slices of cucumber and the baguette.

about 510 kcal/2130 kJ

Pork Fillet in Vegetable Sauce

350 g/12 oz pork fillet, salt and freshly ground pepper, 30 ml/2 tbsp butter or margarine

2 kohlrabi, 300 g/11 oz carrots

250 ml/8 fl oz/1 cup vegetable stock (instant) or vegetable purée (paste)

90 ml/6 tbsp soured (dairy sour) cream

1 bunch flat-leafed parsley, 4 slices baguette

1. Cut the pork into slices about 2 cm/¾ in thick and season on both sides with salt and pepper. Melt the fat in a frying pan on a medium heat and fry the fillet slices for 3-4 minutes on each side. Then wrap in aluminium foil and place on one side.
2. Peel the kohlrabi and the carrots and grate finely. Fry in the frying pan for 2-3 minutes.
3. Add the vegetable stock or purée. Season the vegetable sauce with pepper and salt. Cover and leave to simmer on a low heat for about 5 minutes.
4. Stir in the soured cream, then return the fillet slices and cooking juices to the frying pan.
5. Wash the parsley, shake dry and chop finely. Arrange the fillet slices with the vegetable sauce on two plates and sprinkle with the parsley. Serve with the baguette slices.

about 640 kcal/2670 kJ

Smoked Pork Loin with Crispy Potato

300 g/11 oz floury potatoes

30 ml/2 tbsp oil, salt and freshly ground pepper, nutmeg

1 small bunch green sauce herbs or about 1 handful mixed herbs (e.g. parsley, dill (dill weed), chervil, lovel, basil, sorrel, tarragon, marjoram)

30-45 ml/2-3 tbsp cream quark, 30 ml/2 tbsp soured (dairy sour) cream, 15 ml/1 tbsp lemon juice

100 g/4 oz smoked pork loin, sliced

1. Peel the potatoes, wash and finely grate.

2. Heat the oil in a frying pan. On a medium heat, fry the potatoes, pressing them a little into the base of the pan until golden-brown, about 7 minutes. Turn the crispy potato pancake carefully and fry the other side, also for about 7 minutes. Season well with salt, pepper and nutmeg, and cut into pieces.

3. Meanwhile, wash the herbs, shake dry and chop very finely.

4. To make the herb sauce, stir together the quark, soured cream, lemon juice and herbs. Season with salt and pepper.

5. Serve the smoked pork slices together with the crispy potato pancake and the herb sauce.

about 350 kcal/1460 kJ

Fried Bean Noodles with Pork Fillet

200 g/7 oz pork fillet

25 g/1 oz bean noodles

400 g/14 oz fresh spinach, salt

30 ml/2 tbsp groundnut (peanut) oil,
freshly ground pepper,
1 pinch cayenne pepper,
30 ml/2 tbsp soy sauce

50 g/2 oz/½ cup cashew nuts

1. Bring a large saucepan full of water to the boil.
2. Meanwhile, cut the pork fillet into thin slices and halve the larger slices.
3. Pour 500 ml/17 fl oz/2¼ cups of the boiling water over the bean noodles in a bowl to swell, following the instructions on the packet.
4. Pick out the best of the spinach and wash thoroughly. Salt the remaining cooking water. Cook the spinach for about 1 minute until it falls apart. Then rinse in a sieve with cold water, drain and squeeze well with a wooden spoon.

5. Heat the oil in a frying pan (skillet). Fry the pork fillets on all sides. During cooking, season with salt and pepper, soy sauce and cayenne pepper. Remove the meat from the frying pan and place on a warm plate to keep warm.
6. Lightly fry the spinach. Drain the bean noodles and fry on a medium heat for just a short time. Finally return the pork to the frying pan, mix everything together and season once more.
7. Before serving, sprinkle with the cashew nuts.

about 510 kcal/2130 kJ

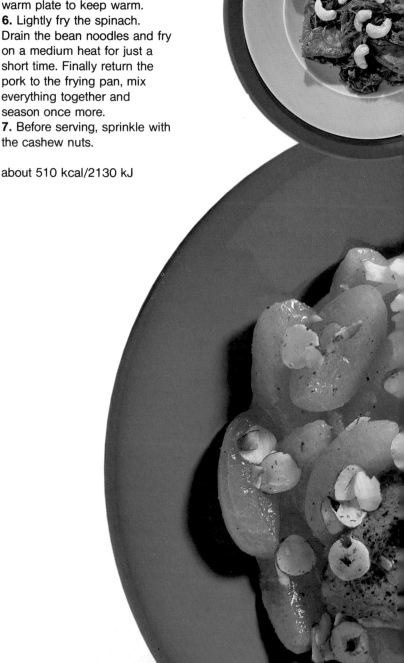

Pork Fillet with Apricots

100 g/4 oz/½ cup quick-cooking rice, salt

1 small can apricot halves,
25 g/1 oz/¼ cup hazelnut flakes

300 g/11 oz pork fillet, freshly ground pepper, 15 ml/1 tbsp butter

ground ginger, ground allspice, lemon juice

1. Cook the rice in salted water, following the instructions on the packet.

2. Meanwhile, drain the apricots in a sieve and halve again. Fry the hazelnuts without fat in a frying pan (skillet) until golden-brown.

3. Cut the pork fillet into slices about 2 cm/¾ in thick and season on each side with pepper. On a high heat, fry both sides in the butter for 3-4 minutes, then add salt.

4. Add the apricots and season to taste with ginger, allspice and lemon juice Cover and simmer on a mild heat for about 5 minutes.

5. Season the apricot sauce with salt and pepper. Arrange the fillet slices with the sauce and rice on two plates, and sprinkle with hazelnuts.

about 495 kcal/2070 kJ

Beef Fillet in Beetroot Cream

150 g/15 oz mild pickled beetroot

1 small onion, 1 pickled gherkin

250 g/9 oz beef fillet

15 ml/1 tbsp butter, salt and freshly ground pepper

100 g/4 oz/½ cup quick-cooking rice

5 ml/1 tsp tomato purée (paste),
5 ml/1 tsp medium-hot mustard,
150 g/5 oz/⅔ cup crème fraîche

15 ml/1 tbsp brandy

1. Leave the beetroot to drain in a sieve and then dice small.
2. Peel the onion and chop finely. Dice the gherkin.
3. Remove the fat from the beef fillet. Cut the meat into narrow strips.
4. Heat the butter and fry the meat a few strips at a time. Remove, salt and pepper, and keep warm.

5. Then fry the diced beetroot, onion and gherkin in the remaining frying juices for about 5 minutes.
6. Prepare the rice, following the instructions on the packet.
7. Add the tomato purée, mustard and crème fraîche to the beetroot and simmer for about 5 minutes.
8. Season the sauce with salt and pepper, and add the brandy. Return the meat strips and the cooking juices to the sauce for about 1 minute. Serve with the rice.

about 690 kcal/2880 kJ

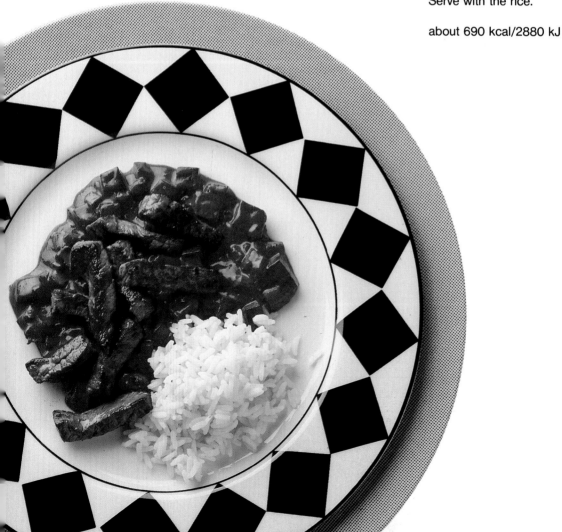

Beef Fillets with Mango Sauce

2 slices beef fillet, each weighing
150 g/5 oz,
freshly ground pepper,
5 ml/1 tsp medium-hot mustard

1 fresh green chilli pepper,
30 ml/2 tbsp oil,
100 g/4 oz/½ cup quick-cooking rice,
250 ml/8 fl oz/1 cup vegetable stock
(instant), salt

1 ripe mango, 5 ml/1 tsp lemon juice,
5 ml/1 tsp raspberry vinegar, some
grated rind of an unwaxed lemon

1. Rub pepper and mustard into each side of the fillet slices. Cover and leave to stand for a few minutes.
2. Slit the chilli along the length and remove the seeds with a knife. Then cut the chilli into fine strips. Heat 15 ml/1 tbsp of oil in a saucepan and fry the chilli strips for a short time. Add the rice and fry for 2-3 minutes, stirring all the time. Add the vegetable stock and salt, and cook the rice on a low heat for about 8-10 minutes. Add more stock as required.
3. Heat the remaining oil in a frying pan (skillet) and fry the fillet slices on each side for 4 minutes. Afterwards, season with a little salt.
4. Meanwhile, carefully peel the mango, cut the fruit flesh from the stone and purée with a hand blender in a bowl. Season the mango purée with the lemon juice, raspberry vinegar and lemon rind.
5. Serve the fillet slices with the chilli rice and mango sauce.

about 440 kcal/1840 kJ

Fried Rice with Beef Fillet

100 g/4 oz/½ cup quick-cooking rice,
salt

1 onion, 250 g/9 oz beef fillet

15 ml/1 tbsp oil

5 ml/1 tsp curry powder

1 small can apricot halves,
15 ml/1 tbsp raisins

2.5 ml/½ tsp turmeric powder, freshly
ground pepper

1. Cook the rice, following the
instructions on the packet.
2. Meanwhile, peel the onion
and cut into segments. Cut the
beef fillet into thin strips.
3. Heat half the oil in a frying
pan (skillet) and fry the meat for
about 3 minutes until brown,
stirring all the time. Then
remove from the heat, cover
and keep warm.

4. Heat the remaining oil and fry
the onion for about 3 minutes,
then sprinkle with the curry
powder.
5. Over a bowl, drain the apricot
halves in a sieve. Add the juice
and the raisins to the onions.
Simmer for about 5 minutes on
a low heat.

6. Halve the apricot halves, add
them to the onions and add the
boiled rice and fillet strips. Heat
everything once more.
7. Season with turmeric, salt
and pepper and curry powder.

about 555 kcal/2320 kJ

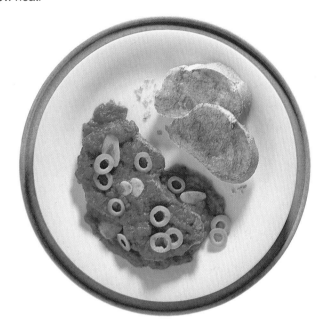

Tomato Steak

2 rump steaks, each weighing 150 g/
5 oz, salt and freshly ground pepper

45-60 ml/3-4 tbsp olive oil

2 cloves garlic, 1-2 cartons chopped
tomatoes, each weighing
500 g/1¼ lb, 5 ml/1 tsp dried
oregano

4 thin slices baguette

10 green olives

1. Remove the fat from around
the edges of the steaks.
Tenderize the meat and season
with salt and pepper.
2. Heat the oil in a frying pan
(skillet) and on a high heat fry
the steaks on each side for
about 2 minutes.
3. Peel the garlic cloves and
slice thinly. Add to the frying
pan and fry for a short time.

Pour the chopped tomato on
top of the steaks and add the
oregano. Cover the pan and
braise for about 20 minutes.
4. Meanwhile, toast the
baguette slices until golden-
brown. Remove the stones from
the olives and slice. Sprinkle the
olives over the tomato steaks
before eating. Serve with the
baguette.
about 510 kcal/2130 kJ

Courgette and Minced Meat

2 courgettes (zucchini)

60 ml/4 tbsp oil

250 g/9 oz minced (ground) beef

salt and freshly ground pepper,
5 ml/1 tsp dried basil,
5 ml/1 tsp dried oregano,
60 ml/4 tbsp lemon juice

2 cartons yoghurt, 2 cloves garlic

4 slices baguette,
15 ml/1 tbsp butter

1. Wash the courgettes and cut off the ends. Slice the vegetables first along the length, then cut across in strips.
2. Next heat 30 ml/2 tbsp of oil in a frying pan (skillet) and fry the courgette strips until firm to the bite. Remove the vegetable and place on one side.
3. Heat the remaining oil and fry the minced meat on a medium heat for 4-5 minutes, until it is light brown and crumbly, stirring all the time.
4. Stir in the courgette strips and season with the spices and the lemon juice. Simmer the vegetables for about 3 minutes.
5. Meanwhile, crush the garlic cloves. Season the yoghurt with salt and pepper, the garlic cloves and the rest of the lemon juice.
6. Arrange the courgettes and minced meat on two plates with the baguette slices spread with butter.

about 955 kcal/3990 kJ

Chinese Cabbage Stir-Fry

1 small Chinese cabbage

1 clove garlic, 30 ml/2 tbsp oil,
250 g/9 oz minced (ground) beef,
salt

30 ml/2 tbsp soy sauce,
15 ml/1 tbsp sherry vinegar

100 g/4 oz/½ cup quick-cooking rice

ground ginger, 2 pinches ground coriander (cilantro), cayenne pepper

1. Cut the Chinese cabbage in half along the length, wash and shake dry. Remove the stalk inside. Cut across the cabbage to make thin strips.
2. Peel the garlic clove and cut into fine slices. In a frying pan

Egg Strips with Mushrooms

1 onion, 50 g/2 oz bacon,
15 ml/1 tbsp butter or margarine

1 large can mushrooms,
15 ml/1 tbsp gin,
45 ml/3 tbsp crème fraîche, salt and
freshly ground pepper

4 eggs, nutmeg, 15 ml/1 tbsp oil

1 small bunch parsley

(skillet), fry in the oil until soft. Add the minced meat and stir-fry until light brown, then season with salt.

3. Add the Chinese cabbage, soy sauce and sherry vinegar to the minced meat. Stir-fry everything for 3-4 minutes.

4. Meanwhile, cook the rice following the instructions on the packet.

5. Season the Chinese cabbage, stir-fry with salt, a little ginger and coriander as well as some cayenne pepper, then serve with the rice.

about 590 kcal/2470 kJ

1. Peel the onion and dice finely. Cut the bacon into thin strips. Heat the fat in a frying pan (skillet). First fry the onions until soft, then fry the bacon for a short time.

2. Drain the mushrooms in a sieve. Add them to the frying pan and fry for about 2 minutes. Cover with gin. Stir in the crème fraîche and season

the mushroom cream with salt and pepper.

3. Meanwhile, whisk the eggs with 120 ml/4 fl oz/½ cup of water. Season well with salt, pepper and grated nutmeg. Heat half the oil in a non-stick frying pan (skillet). Pour in half the egg mixture and leave to thicken. Remove and keep warm. Make another egg pancake from the remaining egg mixture and the rest of the oil. Cut the pancakes into strips, then divide between two warmed plates.

4. Wash the parsley, shake dry and chop finely. Mix with the mushroom cream and pour over the egg pancake strips. Serve at once.

about 675 kcal/2820 kJ

Leeks with Bacon and Fried Egg

75 g/3 oz streaky bacon rashers (slices)

400 g/14 oz leeks,
60 ml/3 tbsp vegetable stock (instant),
salt and freshly ground pepper,
nutmeg

2 portions cooked mashed potato,
30 ml/2 tbsp butter

15 ml/1 tbsp oil, 2 eggs

1. Cut the bacon into strips about 2.5 cm/1 in wide and fry in a frying pan (skillet) without fat until crispy. Remove and place on one side. Pour off all but 15 ml/1 tbsp of the fat (do not dispose of it down the sink, but wait until it has gone cold and put it in the waste bin).
2. Clean the leek, wash, cut into rings and fry for 2 minutes in the bacon fat. Add the stock and fry for about 5 minutes on a low heat. Season with salt and pepper and grated nutmeg.
3. Meanwhile, heat through the mashed potato with the butter.
4. Heat the oil in a second frying pan and fry the eggs.
5. Mix the fried bacon with the leeks. Serve with the potato and the fried eggs.

about 475 kcal/1990 kJ

Herb Spaghetti with Bacon

50 g/2 oz streaky bacon, diced

1 small can sauerkraut (cooked),
5 ml/1 tsp caraway seeds,
1 bay leaf, 3 juniper berries

120 ml/4 fl oz/1 cup vegetable stock (instant)

150 g/5 oz egg spaghetti

5 ml/1 tsp butter or margarine

salt and freshly ground pepper

1. Fry the bacon until crispy.
2. Add the sauerkraut, caraway seeds, bay leaf and juniper berries.
3. Pour the stock into the saucepan and simmer uncovered, for about 10 minutes.
4. Meanwhile, cook the spaghetti, following the instructions on the packet. Drain well.
5. Heat the butter or margarine in a frying pan (skillet) and brown the spaghetti.
6. Mix the spaghetti with the sauerkraut and season with salt and pepper.

about 520 kcal/2170 kJ

Minced Meat Balls with Yoghurt Sauce

300 g/11 oz mixed minced (ground) meat

1 egg, salt, freshly ground pepper,
5 ml/1 tsp dried oregano,
5 ml/1 tsp dried basil

1 bunch parsley

50 g/2 oz/½ cup grated Parmesan cheese

15 ml/1 tbsp oil

200 g/7 oz young spinach

1 carton Greek sheep's milk yoghurt
(200 g/7 oz/1 cup),
1 clove garlic, cayenne pepper,
30 ml/2 tbsp lemon juice,
1 pinch sugar,
4 slices baguette

1. In a bowl, knead the minced meat together with the egg and season with the spices.
2. Wash the parsley, shake dry and chop finely. Knead into the meat dough together with the Parmesan cheese. With wet hands, shape the mixture into tiny balls.
3. Heat the oil in a frying pan (skillet) and fry the little minced balls all over for 10-15 minutes until brown.

4. Meanwhile, clean the spinach, wash thoroughly and briefly bring it to the boil. Rinse the spinach in cold water in a sieve and squeeze well. Then chop coarsely.
5. Crush the garlic clove. Season the yoghurt with the garlic, as well as the salt and pepper, cayenne pepper, lemon juice and sugar. Stir in the spinach and serve the baguette with the sauce and the little minced meat balls.

about 640 kcal/2670 kJ

Chicken Breast with Dill Cucumber

1 cucumber

15 ml/1 tbsp butter or margarine, salt

2 chicken breasts, freshly ground pepper, 15 ml/1 tbsp oil

50 g/2 oz wholemeal noodles

1 bunch dill (dill weed), 15 ml/1 tbsp crème fraîche, curry powder

1. Peel the cucumber and halve along the length. Remove the seeds with a spoon and cut the cucumber halves into slices about 1 cm/ ½ in thick.

2. Heat the fat in a saucepan and stir-fry the cucumber slices for about 3 minutes. Season with some salt. Cover the saucepan and braise on a low heat for about 8 minutes.

3. Meanwhile, season the chicken breast fillets with salt and pepper. On a medium heat, fry both sides in hot oil for about 4-5 minutes.

4. Cook the noodles in salted water until *al dente*.

5. Wash the dill, shake dry and chop finely. Stir the dill and the crème fraîche into the cucumber and season with some pepper and curry powder.

6. Arrange the cucumber, chicken breast fillets and noodles on two plates.

about 340 kcal/1420 kJ

Vegetable and Turkey Main Course Soup

750 ml/1¼ pt/3 cups chicken stock

juice of 1 small lemon

100 g/4 oz turkey slice

100 g/4 oz mangetout (snow peas)

250 g/9 oz green asparagus

50 g/2 oz soup noodles

salt and freshly ground pepper, nutmeg

2 egg yolks

1 small bunch fresh basil

1. Heat the chicken stock in a large saucepan and leave to simmer on a medium heat.

2. Pour half the lemon juice into the chicken stock.

3. Remove the skin and fat from the turkey slice. Cut the meat into 2 cm/¾ in cubes.

4. Wash and clean the mangetout. Wash the asparagus and cut off the woody ends. Cut the asparagus into 5 cm/2 in lengths.

5. On a low heat, cook the asparagus in the soup for about 5 minutes.

6. Add the mangetout and the soup noodles, and simmer for about 3 minutes. Then add the diced turkey and simmer for another 3 minutes.

7. Season the vegetable dish with salt and pepper and grated nutmeg.

8. Whisk the egg yolks in a bowl, adding the remaining lemon juice and 30-45 ml/2-3 tbsp of soup.

9. Remove the saucepan from the heat and pour in the whisked egg yolks, stirring all the time.

10. Wash the basil leaves, shake dry, chop finely and sprinkle over the soup.

about 240 kcal/1000 kJ

Chicken in Red Wine

75 g/3 oz smoked streaky bacon,
1 bunch spring onions (scallions)

3 chicken breast fillets, salt and
freshly ground pepper

15 ml/1 tbsp butter, 15 ml/1 tbsp
flour

120 ml/4 fl oz/½ cup red wine,
1 bay leaf,
1 small sprig rosemary,
dried thyme

1 bunch parsley, nutmeg

1 pinch sugar

4 slices white bread

1. Cut the bacon into short strips. Wash the spring onions well, clean and cut into walnut-sized pieces.
2. Dice the chicken breast fillets and season with salt and pepper. Fry the bacon in a saucepan until transparent.
3. Add the butter to the bacon and stir-fry the spring onions and the chicken meat. Sprinkle with the flour and braise for about 3 minutes. Add the wine, the bay leaf and the herbs. Cover and pot roast for about 15 minutes.

4. Wash the parsley, shake dry and chop finely. Season the red wine and chicken with salt and pepper, grated nutmeg and sugar. Sprinkle with parsley.
5. Toast the bread until golden-brown and serve with the chicken.

about 590 kcal/2470 kJ

Chicken with Summer Vegetables

2 chicken legs, salt and freshly ground pepper

15-30 ml/1-2 tbsp oil,
120 ml/4 fl oz/½ cup dry white wine

1 packet frozen summer vegetables (300 g/11 oz)

100 g/4 oz/½ cup quick-cooking rice, 2 bunches parsley

120 ml/4 fl oz/½ cup single (light) cream, 2.5 ml/½ tsp cornflour (cornstarch), 30 ml/2 tbsp white wine

1. Rinse the chicken legs and pat dry. Rub in salt and pepper.

2. Heat the oil in a large saucepan and fry the chicken until golden-brown. Pour in three-quarters of the dry white wine, cover and cook the chicken on a low heat for about 15 minutes. Remove the chicken and place on one side.

3. Place the vegetables in the saucepan and fry for a short time in the frying juices. Lay the chicken on top, add the remaining wine and cook for another 15 minutes.

4. Meanwhile, cook the quick cooking rice, following the instructions on the packet. Wash the parsley, shake dry and chop finely.

5. Just before the chicken is cooked, stir the cream into the saucepan. Stir together the cornflour and the 30 ml/2 tbsp of wine until smooth. Stirring all the time, pour into the saucepan. Bring everything to the boil.

6. Arrange the chicken together with the vegetables and the rice on two plates. Sprinkle with the parsley.

about 710 kcal/2970 kJ

Duck Breast with Mushroom Risotto

1 duck breast, salt and freshly ground pepper

150 g/5 oz oyster mushrooms, 1 small onion, 15 ml/1 tbsp butter or margarine

50 g/2 oz/¼ cup quick-cooking rice, 120 ml/4 fl oz/½ cup meat stock

50 g/2 oz/½ cup grated Parmesan cheese

1. Make diagonal cuts in the duck breast on the skin side. Salt and pepper the meat. On a medium heat, heat a frying pan (skillet) without fat and fry the duck breast on the fat side for about 10 minutes; turn over and fry for another 5-8 minutes. Wrap in aluminium foil and set aside.
2. Briefly wash the oyster mushrooms, pat dry and cut into strips. Peel the onion and dice small. Heat half the fat in a saucepan and lightly fry the mushrooms and the onion.
3. Add the rice and fry for a short time. Pour in the stock and cook for about 8 minutes on a low heat.
4. Carefully season the risotto with salt and pepper, Parmesan cheese and the remaining butter or margarine.
5. Remove the duck breast from the aluminium foil and cut into diagonal slices. Arrange with the mushroom risotto on two plates.

about 640 kcal/2670 kJ

Chicken Breast with Green Pea Sauce

150 g/5 oz frozen peas

50 g/2 oz/¼ cup quick-cooking rice, salt

60 ml/2 tbsp soured (dairy sour) cream

freshly ground pepper, cayenne pepper, 5 ml/1 tsp lemon juice, Worcestershire sauce

2 chicken breast fillets, 5 ml/1 tsp oil

1. Bring the peas with 100 ml/ 3½ fl oz/6½ tbsp of water to the boil and simmer for about 5 minutes on a low heat. Remove 60 ml/2 tbsp of peas and set aside.
2. Meanwhile, cook the rice in salted water, following the instructions on the packet.
3. Stir 30 ml/1 tbsp of soured cream into the cooked peas in the saucepan, then purée with a hand blender.
4. Season the sauce with the spices, lemon juice and a dash of Worcestershire sauce, and keep warm.
5. Lightly pepper the chicken breast fillets. Heat the oil in a frying pan (skillet), fry the fillets over a medium heat for about 3 minutes on each side, then season with salt.
6. Mix the reserved peas with the rice. Arrange the chicken breasts together with the rice and the green pea sauce on two plates. Place 5 ml/1 tsp of soured cream on each portion of green pea sauce.

about 375 kcal/1570 kJ

Chicken Liver and Broccoli Fry

300 g/11 oz frozen broccoli, salt

200 g/7 oz chicken liver,
30 ml/2 tbsp flour,
freshly ground pepper

30 ml/2 tbsp butter or margarine

2 shallots,
about 120 ml/4 fl oz/½ cup Marsala

dried oregano, 4 slices baguette

1. Cook the broccoli in salted water for about 10 minutes. Then drain in a sieve.
2. Meanwhile, clean the chicken liver. Season the flour with salt and pepper. Toss the chicken liver in the flour.
3. In the frying pan (skillet), melt 1 tbsp of fat until it foams. Fry the chicken liver on each side for 2-3 minutes. Remove, set aside on a plate, covered.

4. Peel the shallots, chop finely and fry in the juices, stirring until transparent. Pour in the Marsala and cook briefly. Remove the frying pan from the heat and stir in the remaining tablespoon of butter or margarine. Season with salt and pepper and oregano.
5. Return the chicken liver to the frying pan and cook for another 3-5 minutes on a low heat. Serve together with the broccoli and baguette.

about 550 kcal/2300 kJ

Fish
and
Vegetables

Trout with Nut Butter

2 ready-to-cook trout, salt and freshly ground pepper

1 bunch flat-leafed parsley

60 ml/4 tbsp butter at room temperature

15 ml/1 tbsp hazelnut or almond flakes or coarsely chopped nuts, ½ lime or ½ unwaxed lemon

2 portions mashed potato (ready-made, about 50 g/2 oz powder), nutmeg

1. Wash the trout under running water and pat dry on absorbent kitchen paper. Rub the fish inside and out with salt and pepper.
2. Wash the parsley and shake dry. Break off the thick stalks and place one stalk in ecah of the trout. Reserve the parsley leaves.
3. Heat 30 ml/2 tbsp of butter in a large frying pan (skillet). Fry the trout on each side for about 4 minutes on a low to medium heat.

4. Meanwhile, with a fork mix the remaining butter with the nuts. Season with salt, a little grated lime or lemon rind and some lime or lemon juice.
5. Pour the frying juices out of the frying pan. Add the nut butter to the trout in the frying pan and melt on a low heat.
6. Prepare the mashed potato, following the instructions on the packet and season with grated nutmeg.
7. Arrange the trout together with the nut butter and the mashed potato on two plates. Garnish with the parsley leaves.

about 600 kcal/2510 kJ

Salmon with Tarragon Cream in a Potato Coating

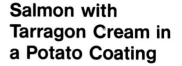

300 g/11 oz salmon fillet or 400 g/14 oz salmon cutlets, freshly ground pepper, 15 ml/1 tbsp lemon juice

a few sprigs tarragon or dill (dill weed), 45 ml/3 tbsp crème fraîche, salt

200 g/7 oz potatoes, 1 small egg white, nutmeg

1. Preheat the oven to 240°C/475°F/gas mark 9. Remove the skin from the salmon fillet, if necessary, and remove the skin and the large bones in the centre of the cutlets. Then season the salmon with pepper, place in a gratin dish and sprinkle with lemon juice.
2. Chop the tarragon or the dill finely. Stir into the crème fraîche and season with salt and pepper. Spread over the salmon.
3. Peel the potatoes and grate coarsely. Stir in the egg white and season well with salt and pepper and grated nutmeg.
4. Spread the potato mixture over the salmon and bake for about 25 minutes until golden-brown.
A fresh leaf salad goes well with this dish.

about 415 kcal/1735 kJ

Squid and Tomato Stir-Fry

500 g/1 lb frozen squid

4 small tomatoes, 1 bunch coriander (cilantro) or flat-leafed parsley

1 lime, 1 clove garlic, 1 dried chilli pepper

45 ml/3 tbsp olive oil

salt and freshly ground pepper

4 slices baguette

1. Defrost the squid in a saucepan on a medium heat for about 10 minutes.

2. Meanwhile, wash the tomatoes and halve them. Wash the coriander or the parsley, shake dry and chop finely.

3. Grate the lime rind and squeeze the lime juice. Peel the garlic and chop finely. Cut the chilli pepper open along the length, remove the seeds and chop finely.

4. Pat the squid dry with absorbent kitchen paper and cut into walnut-sized pieces.

5. Heat the olive oil in a frying pan (skillet) and on a high heat, stir-fry the squid for 3 minutes, stirring all the time. Add the lime juice, garlic, chilli and tomatoes, and pot roast everything for a further 5 minutes.

6. Finally stir in the salt and pepper and lime rind along with the herbs. Serve together with the baguette.

about 520 kcal/2170 kJ

Prawns with Spinach and Cream Sauce

1 small onion,
15 ml/1 tbsp butter or margarine

300 g/11 oz frozen leaf spinach

100 ml/3½ fl oz/6½ tbsp soured (dairy sour) cream

1 clove garlic, salt, cayenne pepper

300 g/11 oz prawns (shrimps) (with shell)

15 ml/1 tbsp olive oil

freshly ground pepper, nutmeg, 15 ml/1 tbsp lemon juice

1. Peel the onion and chop finely. Heat the fat and fry the onion until transparent.
2. Then add the frozen spinach and cook for about 10 minutes on a low heat.
3. Crush the garlic clove. Mix with the soured cream, salt and some cayenne pepper.
4. Heat the olive oil and fry the prawns on both sides for about 3 minutes.
5. Season the spinach with salt, pepper, grated nutmeg and lemon juice, and serve with the prawns and soured cream.

about 350 kcal/1460 kJ

Plaice Fillets with Shallot Butter

100 g/4 oz/½ cup long-grain rice (wild rice mixture), salt

2 plaice fillets,
15 ml/1 tbsp butter or margarine

1 shallot, 30 ml/2 tbsp dry white wine, 30 ml/2 tbsp cold butter

10 ml/2 tsp lumpfish caviar,
1 sprig dill (dill weed)

1. Cook the rice in a scant 250 ml/8 fl oz/1 cup of salt water, following the instructions on the packet.
2. Meanwhile, season the plaice fillets with salt. Heat the butter or margarine in a frying pan (skillet) and fry the fillets on a low heat for 2-3 minutes on each side. Remove the fish fillets from the frying pan and keep warm on a plate.
3. Peel the shallot and dice finely. On a low heat, fry in the cooking juices from the fish until soft. (Under no circumstances fry them until they are brown!) Add the wine and simmer for a while, reducing the liquid. Then remove the frying pan from the heat and whisk in the cold butter. Season the shallot butter with a little salt.
4. Arrange the plaice fillets with the shallot butter, the rice and the caviar on two plates. Decorate with a sprig of washed dill.

about 425 kcal/1780 kJ

Spaghetti with Tuna Fish

150 g/5 oz spaghetti, salt

1 large onion, 2 cloves garlic, 1 green chilli pepper, 30 ml/2 tbsp oil

1 can tuna fish in its own juice, 60 ml/4 tbsp crème fraîche

4 tomatoes

some cress

1. Cook the spaghetti until *al dente* in salted water.
2. Meanwhile, peel the onion and cut into fine strips. Peel the garlic and chop very finely. Cut the chilli pepper into rings, and remove the seeds. Heat the oil in a frying pan (skillet) and braise the onion, garlic and chilli, stirring all the time.

3. Drain the tuna fish and break up the chunks with two forks. Add to the frying pan and fry for 3-4 minutes. Stir in the crème fraîche.
4. Wash the tomatoes, dice finely and add to the tuna fish sauce.
5. Drain the spaghetti in a sieve and arrange on two plates. Pour on the sauce and sprinkle with some washed and chopped cress.

about 650 kcal/2720 kJ

Green Noodles in Aubergine Sauce

1 small onion, 3 cloves garlic,
1 small aubergine (eggplant)

30 ml/2 tbsp olive oil

120 ml/4 fl oz/½ cup vegetable
stock (instant)

200 g/7 oz green noodles, salt

30 ml/1 tbsp wine vinegar, freshly
ground pepper

30 ml/2 tbsp butter,
50 g/2 oz/½ cup grated Parmesan
cheese

1. Peel the onion and the
garlic cloves and chop both
finely. Wash the aubergine,
clean and dice finely.

2. Heat the oil in a saucepan.
Fry the diced onion, garlic and
aubergine for about 5 minutes.
3. Add the stock and simmer
for about 10 minutes.
4. Meanwhile, cook the
noodles until *al dente*. Then
drain in a sieve.
5. Season the aubergine
sauce with the wine vinegar,
salt and pepper. Divide the
noodles between two plates
and pour on the sauce.
6. Top each portion with half
the butter and Parmesan
cheese.

about 765 kcal/3200 kJ

Gnocchi with Herb Sauce

1 small onion, 15 ml/1 tbsp butter or
margarine, 1 carton single (light)
cream

1 bunch sorrel, 1 bunch chervil, salt
and freshly ground pepper, cayenne
pepper, 15 ml/1 tbsp lemon juice

500 g/1 lb gnocchi (dumplings
made of potato dough, ready-made)

1. Peel the onion and chop
finely. Heat the fat in a
saucepan and braise the onion
on a medium heat until
transparent. Add the cream
and cook for 5-7 minutes on a
medium heat.

2. Wash the herbs, shake dry,
chop coarsely and add to the
cream. Purée the sauce with a
hand blender and season with
salt, pepper, cayenne pepper
and lemon juice.
3. Prepare the gnocchi in
boiling salted water, following
the instructions on the packet.
Drain and mix with the sauce.

about 665 kcal/2780 kJ

Wholemeal Spaghetti with Leek Sauce

150 g/5 oz wholemeal spaghetti, salt

300 g/11 oz frozen leeks with cream

1 small clove garlic, 15 ml/1 tbsp cream, 15 ml/1 tbsp grated Parmesan cheese, freshly ground pepper, some lemon juice

1 small bunch parsley

1. Cook the spaghetti in salted water until *al dente*.

2. Meanwhile, defrost the frozen leeks in a little water and cook on a low heat, following the instructions on the packet.

3. Peel the garlic clove and crush it in a garlic press over the leeks. Stir in the cream and the grated cheese. Season the sauce well with salt and pepper and lemon juice.

4. Wash the parsley, shake dry and chop finely. Stir into the leek sauce.

5. Drain the spaghetti in a sieve and serve together with the leek sauce.

about 650 kcal/2720 kJ

Red Spaghetti with Herb Sauce

300 ml/1½ pt/1¼ cups beetroot (beet) juice, 5 ml/1 tsp salt, 150 g/5 oz spaghetti

1 small pickled gherkin, 1 shallot, 1 bunch dill (dill weed)

250 g/9 oz/1 cup soured (dairy sour) cream, 60 ml/2 tbsp single (light) cream, freshly ground pepper, some lemon juice, sugar

1. Boil the beetroot juice with 1.5 l/2½ pt/6 cups of water and the salt. Add the spaghetti and cook until *al dente*.

2. Meanwhile, dice the pickled gherkin. Peel the shallot and dice, wash the dill, shake dry and chop.

3. With a hand blender, purée the gherkin, shallot and dill together with half the soured cream. Stir in the remaining soured cream and the single cream. Season the sauce with salt, pepper, lemon juice and sugar.

4. Drain the spaghetti in a sieve and arrange together with the herb sauce on two plates.

about 465 kcal/1940 kJ

Spinach Noodles with Gorgonzola Cream

150 g/5 oz green noodles, salt

5 ml/1 tsp butter or margarine

200 g/7 oz Gorgonzola cheese

60 ml/4 tbsp single (light) cream, freshly ground pepper, nutmeg

1 small bunch parsley, 6 walnut halves

1. Cook the noodles in well-salted water until *al dente*.
2. Meanwhile, melt the butter in a saucepan on a low heat. Cut the cheese into pieces and melt in the butter, stirring all the time. Pour in the cream and mix it with the cheese to make a creamy sauce. Season with pepper and grated nutmeg.
3. Wash the parsley and shake dry. Coarsely chop the parsley and walnuts.
4. Drain the noodles. Arrange on two plates and pour over the Gorgonzola cream. Then sprinkle with the chopped parsley and nuts.

about 790 cal/3300 kJ

Tortellini in Rosemary Sauce

250 g/10 oz tortellini with meat filling (ready-made), salt

30 ml/2 tbsp butter or margarine

60 ml/4 tbsp crème fraîche, 60 ml/4 tbsp single (light) cream, freshly ground pepper

3-4 small sprigs rosemary

Worcestershire sauce, cayenne pepper

1. Cook the tortellini in salted water.
2. Meanwhile, melt the butter in a saucepan, add the crème fraîche and cream and whisk

Red Spaghetti with Caper Pesto

together well. Bring to the boil. Season with salt and pepper.

3. Tear the leaves from the washed rosemary sprigs, finely chop and stir into the sauce.

4. Rinse the tortellini through a sieve, drain well and cook in the sauce for 3-4 minutes on a low heat.

5. Season the pasta dish with a dash of Worcestershire sauce and some cayenne pepper.

about 410 kcal/1710 kJ

---

250 g/9 oz red spaghetti, salt

---

45 ml/3 tbsp capers, 30 ml/2 tbsp sunflower seeds, 5 ml/1 tsp green peppercorns, 1 bunch parsley, 100 g/4 oz mozzarella cheese

---

30 ml/2 tbsp orange juice, 30 ml/2 tbsp balsamic vinegar, 60 ml/4 tbsp olive oil, 5 ml/1 tsp crème fraîche, 5 ml/1 tsp medium-hot mustard, 5 ml/1 tsp grated horseradish, freshly ground pepper, 1 pinch sugar

---

1. Cook the spaghetti in salted water until *al dente*.

2. Meanwhile, purée the

capers, sunflower seeds, green peppercorns, washed and coarsely chopped parsley and the diced mozzarella cheese with a hand blender or food processor.

3. Place the purée in a bowl and stir in the orange juice, balsamic vinegar, olive oil and the crème fraîche. Then season with mustard, horseradish, salt, pepper and sugar.

4. Drain the spaghetti in a sieve and then serve with the pesto.

about 860 kcal/3590 kJ

Fennel Escalope with Lemon Rice

1 large fennel bulb,
salt and freshly ground pepper,
nutmeg

1 egg,
50 g/2 oz/½ cup breadcrumbs

30 ml/2 tbsp butter or margarine

100 g/4 oz/½ cup quick-cooking
rice,
2.5 ml/½ tsp grated lemon rind

100 g/4 oz Gorgonzola cheese

lemon juice to taste

1. Wash the fennel, clean and cut into finger-thick slices along the length. Rub with salt, pepper and grated nutmeg.
2. Beat the egg in a bowl. Dip the fennel slices on both sides in the egg, then coat in breadcrumbs.
3. Heat the butter and fry the fennel escalope on each side for about 8 minutes.
4. Meanwhile, prepare the rice, following the instructions on the packet. Season with lemon rind and pepper.
5. As the rice is cooking, place pieces of Gorgonzola on the fennel slices and melt in a covered pan.
6. Arrange the fennel schnitzel with the lemon rice on two plates. Sprinkle with lemon juice to taste. Serve the schnitzel immediately.

about 660 kcal/2750 kJ

Boiled Potatoes and Chopped Egg

500 g/1 lb small potatoes, salt

3 hard-boiled (hard-cooked) eggs,
1 small pickled gherkin, ½ bunch
radishes

100 g/4 oz/½ cup crème fraîche,
5 ml/1 tsp grated horseradish,
5 ml/1 tsp medium-hot mustard
freshly ground pepper

1 small bunch chives

1. Wash the potatoes
thoroughly and boil in lightly
salted water for about 20
minutes.
2. Meanwhile, shell the eggs
and chop finely. Dice the
gherkin finely. Wash the
radishes and grate coarsely.
3. Mix the crème fraîche with
the horseradish, mustard, salt
and pepper. Add the eggs,
gherkin and radishes.

4. Wash the chives, shake dry,
cut into little rolls and add to
the chopped egg.
5. Drain the potatoes and
remove the skins carefully.
Serve on two plates with the
chopped egg.

about 480 kcal/2000 kJ

Couscous with Winter Vegetables

1 small red onion,
1 clove garlic, 1 medium-sized carrot, 1 stick celery

15 ml/1 tbsp butter

150 g/5 oz couscous,
about 250 ml/8 fl oz/1 cup vegetable stock, salt

75 g/3 oz Gorgonzola cheese, freshly ground pepper

1. Peel the onion and chop coarsely. Peel the garlic clove and crush it in a garlic press over the diced onion. Clean the carrot, wash and slice thinly. Wash the celery, pull off the strings and cut into slices. Set aside the celery leaves.
2. Melt the butter in a saucepan and braise the vegetables.
3. Wash the couscous, drain and add to the vegetables. Pour over the stock, season with salt and cook, covered, on a low heat for about 20 minutes. If required, add more stock.
4. Cut the cheese into pieces and stir into the vegetable and millet mixture. Season the mixture with pepper. Finely chop the celery leaves and sprinkle on top.

about 480 kcal/2000 kJ

Wild Rice Risotto with Oyster Mushrooms

3 spring onions (scallions),
1 clove garlic

15 ml/1 tbsp oil,
100 g/4 oz/½ cup long-grain rice (wild rice mixture)

400 ml/14 fl oz/1¾ cups chicken stock, 1 bay leaf,
2.5 ml/½ tsp dried thyme,
2.5 ml/½ tsp dried marjoram,
salt and freshly ground pepper

200 g/7 oz oyster mushrooms,
45 ml/3 tbsp butter or margarine

25 g/1 oz/¼ cup grated Parmesan cheese, 30 ml/2 tbsp lemon juice

fresh basil leaves

1. Clean the spring onions, wash and cut diagonally into slices. Peel the garlic clove and chop finely.
2. Heat the oil in a saucepan and fry the garlic and spring onions, stirring all the time. Then add the rice and briefly cook it.
3. Add the chicken stock, the bay leaf, thyme, marjoram, salt and pepper and cook the risotto on a low heat for about 20 minutes.
4. Clean the oyster mushrooms, wash quickly and pat dry with absorbent kitchen paper. Tear any large mushrooms into strips. Heat 15 ml/1 tbsp of butter or margarine in a frying pan (skillet) and fry the mushrooms until golden-brown.
5. Stir the Parmesan cheese, the remaining butter or margarine and the lemon juice into the cooked risotto.
6. Arrange the risotto together with the oyster mushrooms on two plates and garnish with washed basil leaves.

about 370 kcal/1550 kJ

Courgette Tortilla

300 g/11 oz potatoes, boiled in their skins

1 small onion, 2 small courgettes (zucchini)

45 ml/3 tbsp olive oil,
5 ml/1 tsp dried rosemary,
salt and freshly ground pepper

3 eggs

30 ml/2 tbsp grated Parmesan cheese

1. Peel the boiled potatoes carefully and cut into thin slices (for speed, use an egg slicer).
2. Peel the onion and chop as finely as possible. Clean the courgettes, wash and slice thinly.
3. Heat 15 ml/1 tbsp of olive oil in a non-stick frying pan (skillet) and fry the onion and the courgette for 5-10 minutes. Season with the rosemary, salt and pepper.
4. In a bowl, whisk the eggs, and mix in the potatoes, onions and courgettes.
5. Heat another 15 ml/1 tbsp of olive oil in the frying pan and fry the egg mixture on a gentle heat until golden-brown. Shake the frying pan from time to time, so that nothing sticks.
6. Turn the potato omelette with the aid of a plate and fry the other side with the remaining oil until golden-brown.
7. Halve the tortilla and sprinkle with Parmesan cheese.

about 450 kcal/1880 kJ

Omelette with Bean Sprouts and Chinese Cabbage

3 eggs, 30 ml/2 tbsp milk, salt and freshly ground pepper, paprika

½ cucumber, 100 g/4 oz Chinese cabbage, 50 g/2 oz fresh bean sprouts (e.g. lentil sprouts, alfalfa)

15 ml/1 tbsp lemon juice,
5 ml/1 tsp medium-hot mustard

5 ml/1 tsp oil

1. Whisk the eggs with the milk. Season with salt and pepper, and a little paprika.
2. Wash the cucumber and slice with a grater. Chop the Chinese cabbage into fine strips and rinse in cold water. Blanch the bean sprouts with boiling water.
3. Place the vegetables in a bowl and season with the lemon juice, mustard, salt and pepper.
4. Heat the oil in a frying pan (skillet). Stir the egg mixture and pour into the frying pan. Cover and allow to thicken on a low heat.
5. Slide the finished omelette onto a plate and spread the vegetable mixture on top. Fold and halve. Serve on two plates.

about 135 kcal/565 kJ

Noodle Omelette with Bamboo Shoots

1 large red (bell) pepper,
100 g/4 oz bamboo shoots in strips (canned)

30 ml/2 tbsp oil,
30 ml/2 tbsp sherry vinegar

100 g/4 oz thin Japanese egg noodles, 45-60 ml/3-4 tbsp soy sauce, cayenne pepper

4 eggs

1 bunch coriander (cilantro)

1. Wash the pepper, clean and halve. Remove the white skin and seeds, and cut the pepper into small dice. Drain the bamboo shoots well.
2. Heat the oil in a frying pan (skillet). On a high heat, stir-fry the vegetables for about 5 minutes. Pour in the sherry vinegar.
3. Cook the noodles for about 3 minutes in boiling water,

drain in a sieve and add to the vegetables. Season with the soy sauce and cayenne pepper.
4. Whisk the eggs with 120 ml/4 fl oz/½ cup of water. Remove half the vegetable and noodle mixture from the pan and place on a plate. Spread the remaining mixture evenly over the base of the pan and pour in half of the whisked egg. Cover the pan and leave the omelette to thicken for about 5 minutes on a low heat. Then place it on a plate and keep warm.
5. Prepare the second portion in exactly the same way as above. Finally wash the coriander, shake dry, chop finely and sprinkle over the omelettes. Serve immediately.

about 550 kcal/2300 kJ

Desserts

Peach with Champagne Foam

1 small can peach halves

2 egg yolks, 30 ml/2 tbsp sugar

60-75 ml/4-5 tbsp sparkling dry wine or champagne

1. Drain the peach halves in a sieve.
2. In a bowl (preferably metal), using a hand blender, whisk the egg yolks and sugar until the mixture becomes creamy and light in colour.
3. Then placing the bowl over another filled with hot water (but it must not be boiling), add the champagne or wine a little at a time, beating the crème with a whisk until it is thick and foamy. This will take about 15 minutes.
4. Cut the peach halves into segments. Place the champagne foam on two plates and arrange the peach segments in a fan-like shape.

about 250 kcal/1040 kJ

Melon Carpaccio

500 g/1 lb water melon

100 g/4 oz fresh or frozen raspberries

15 ml/1 tbsp icing (confectioners') sugar
5 ml/1 tsp Campari

1. Cut the melon fruit from the peel and remove the seeds. Then cut the flesh diagonally into thin slices and arrange on two large dessert plates, fan-like.

2. Defrost the raspberries, following the instructions on the packet. Set aside half of them. Purée the rest and pass through a fine sieve.
3. Stir 2 tsp of icing sugar and the Campari into the raspberry purée. Spoon over the melon carpaccio, add the remaining raspberries and sprinkle with icing sugar.

about 245 kcal/1020 kJ

Hot Nougat Pears with Vanilla Ice Cream

50 g/2 oz nougat,
15 ml/1 tbsp milk,
1 pinch cinnamon powder,
15 ml/1 tbsp brandy

1 large ripe pear,
15 ml/1 tbsp lemon juice

4 scoops of vanilla ice cream,
5 ml/1 tsp cocoa powder
(unsweetened chocolate)

1. Preheat the oven to 200°C/400°F/gas mark 6. Meanwhile, cut the nougat into small pieces. Heat the milk in a small bowl set over a bowl of hot water. Add the nougat and cinnamon and let the nougat melt, stirring all the time. Stir in the brandy.
2. Wash the pear and halve. Sprinkle the cut surfaces with lemon juice. Remove the core and widen the hollow a little with a teaspoon, by taking out some of the fruit flesh.
3. Place the pear halves in a soufflé dish and fill the centres with the nougat mixture.

4. Place the pears in the oven on the middle shelf and bake for about 20 minutes. After 5 minutes cover with a sheet of aluminium foil and then continue cooking.
5. Arrange the vanilla ice cream on two plates and place the hot pears alongside. Sprinkle with some cocoa powder.

about 380 kcal/1590 kJ

Pears with Bilberries

1 large aromatic pear,
250 ml/8 fl oz/1 cup medium-sweet white wine

200 g/7 oz fresh or frozen bilberries, sugar, lemon juice, grated rind from an unwaxed lemon, cinnamon powder

15 ml/1 tbsp icing (confectioners') sugar

1. Peel the pear, halve along the length and cut out the core. Lay the pear halves next to each other in a saucepan and add the wine. Bring to the boil, cover and steam the pears on a medium heat for about 15 minutes. Then take them out of the juice and leave to cool on a plate. Reserve the juice.
2. Sort through the fresh bilberries, wash carefully and leave to drain; briefly heat the frozen berries to defrost. Season the bilberries with some sugar, lemon juice, lemon rind and cinnamon.

Purée half the berries with 15-30 ml/1-2 tbsp of the wine juice.
3. Arrange the pear halves together with the bilberries and the bilberry purée on two dessert plates. Sprinkle with icing sugar.

about 150 kcal/630 kJ

Apple Purée with Chocolate Cream

150 g/5 oz double (heavy) cream,
15 ml/1 tbsp rum,
15 ml/1 tbsp cocoa powder
(unsweetened chocolate),
1 pinch cinnamon powder

200 g/7 oz apple purée from a jar

25 g/1 oz chocolate (milk or plain)

1. Whip the cream until stiff. Carefully mix half of it with the rum, cocoa powder and cinnamon.
2. In a dessert bowl, spoon in some apple purée, some chocolate cream, some more apple purée and finally the plain whipped cream. Repeat for the second bowl.
3. Sprinkle grated chocolate over the whipped cream.

about 450 kcal/1880 kJ

Ice Cream with Espresso Zabaglione

5 ml/1 tsp instant espresso coffee powder

10 small almond macaroons (amaretti), 30 ml/2 tbsp amaretto (almond liqueur)

1 egg yolk, 15 ml/1 tbsp sugar

200 g/7 oz vanilla or chocolate ice cream

1. Pour 100 ml/3½ fl oz/6½ tbsp of hot water onto the espresso powder, stir and leave the espresso to cool.
2. Sprinkle the macaroons with the amaretto and set aside.
3. Put the egg yolk in a small bowl, then beat well with the sugar.
4. Add the espresso to the egg and sugar mixture and place the bowl in a bowl of hot water. Using an electric whisk, beat for about 5 minutes until creamy. (Do not let the water come to the boil!)
5. Arrange the ice cream on two dessert plates. Pour over the espresso zabaglione and place the macaroons alongside.

about 390 kcal/1630 kJ

Sharon Fruit and Yoghurt Crème

2 sharon fruit or Japanese
persimmon,
200 g/7 oz yoghurt,
1 pinch sugar,
15-30 ml/1-2 tbsp lemon juice

5 ml/1 tsp honey

15 ml/1 tbsp almond chips

1. Cut the sharon fruit
diagonally through the centre.
Remove the fruit flesh using a
small spoon and place in a
mixing bowl. Add half the
yoghurt and then purée with a
hand blender. Season with a
little sugar and the lemon
juice.
2. Stir the remaining yoghurt
with the honey until smooth.
First pour the fruit yoghurt into
little glass dishes or deep
plates. Then pour the honey
yoghurt in a spiral shape over
it, using a spoon to draw star-
shaped lines through the
dessert. Leave the desserts to
cool for about 15 minutes.
3. Place the almonds in a
frying pan (skillet) without fat
and roast until light brown,
stirring all the time. Sprinkle on
the desserts just before
serving.

about 190 kcal/790 kJ

Peach with Quark Cream

1 small can peach halves in syrup
250 g/9 oz/1 cup quark
1 lime, sugar

1. Drain the peaches in a sieve. Cut two peach halves into thin segments.
2. Cut up the remaining peaches and purée with the quark in a mixer or with a hand blender.

3. Wash and dry the lime. Grate half the rind and squeeze out the lime juice. Season the quark cream with the lime rind and juice, as well as the sugar.
4. Serve the quark cream together with the peach pieces. Garnish with lime peel cut into very thin strips.

about 260 kcal/1090 kJ

Raspberry and Melon Salad

½ honeydew melon, 100 g/4 oz raspberries
15 ml/1 tbsp lemon juice, 2.5 ml/½ tsp sugar
100 g/4 oz double (heavy) cream, 15 ml/1 tbsp Grand Marnier, icing (confectioners') sugar

1. Cut the honeydew melon along the length into segments. Cut off the peel and remove the seeds. Dice the fruit flesh and place in a bowl together with the raspberries.
2. Stir the lemon juice with the sugar and sprinkle over the fruit.
3. Whip the cream until it begins to stiffen, mix in the Grand Marnier, and season with icing sugar to taste.
4. Serve the fruit salad with the cream.

about 270 kcal/1130 kJ

Index

foulsham

The Publishing House
Bennetts Close, Cippenham, Berks SL1 5AP, England.

ISBN 0-572-02050-3

This English language version copyright © 1995 W. Foulsham & Co. Ltd.

Originally published by Falken-Verlag GmbH, Niedernhausen TS, Germany.
Photographs copyright © Falken-Verlag

Title picture: Micharl Brauner, Karlsruhe (Recipe "Chicken with summer vegetables", p. 51).

Photos: Michael Brauner, Karlsruhe: pp 2/3, 4, 5, 6, 7, 8, 9, 10, 11, 12, 13, 16/17 bottom, 18/19 top, 20/21, 22, 24, 26 top, 30, 31, 38/39 bottom, 41, 43, 50, 51, 52, 57, 62/63 right, 64/65 centre, 66/67 left, 68, 72, 74 top, 75, 76/77 left; Peter A. Eising, Munich: pp. 16/17 top, 18 left, 25, 28 bottom, 29 bottom right, 32, 34, 35, 36 bottom, 37, 42, 44 left, 48/49 top, 58, 60/61 centre, 73, 74 bottom, 78; Holz & Wunsch, Cologne: pp. 18/19 bottom, 36 top, 61 right; Ulrich Kerth, Munich: pp. 1, 14 bottom, 33, 40, 55, 56, 59, 60 left, 67 right, 77 right; Thomas von Salomon, Munich: pp. 14 top, 15, 23 top, 26 left, 28/29 top, 38/39 top, 44/45, 45 right, 46 bottom, 47, 48 bottom, 53, 64 left, 65 right, 69, 71, 79; Zuzanna Trnka: pp. 23 bottom, 76/77 right; Friedrich Wondrasch: pp. 27, 46 top, 54, 62 left, 70.

Typeset in Great Britain by Typesetting Solutions, Slough, Berks.

Printed in Great Britain at Cambus Litho, East Kilbride